The New Experimenta in Heilbronn

Edited by
Louisa Hutton and
Matthias Sauerbruch

Texts by
Florian Heilmeyer

T0017186

Lars Müller Publishers

Preface

This slim volume presents the new Experimenta building from three points of view: as one of the most recent episodes in the urban history of Heilbronn; as a piece of architecture with all its spatial, material, functional and technical aspects; and, finally, as a link in the long chain of spiral buildings – an unusual but millennia-old architectural idea that, in the context of diverse cultures and generations, has continually assumed a variety of meanings.

The development of Heilbronn provides a good illustration of the dynamics of smaller European cities away from the metropolises. The settlement by the ford that crossed the river Neckar expanded in the Middle Ages into a free imperial city. It subsequently developed into a nexus – first of trade, then of manufacturing industries with their accompanying mechanisation – so that by the 19th century it was described as a 'Swabian Liverpool'. Almost completely destroyed in the Second World War, Heilbronn was rapidly rebuilt and turned into a modern, car-friendly city that was increasingly absorbed into the sprawl of the wider region due to its extensive offer of mobility. Famous for its metalworking technologies, today even this area – like everywhere in Europe – faces the prospect of fundamental transformation in the face of climate change. The Experimenta building, in fact, is one example of several new structures in Heilbronn that are forging a path towards a future knowledge city.

On the one hand, the new Experimenta building offers robust, high-performance exhibition spaces that are choreographed with a high degree of flexibility and easy orientation. On the other, an 'eye-catcher' was needed that could clearly symbolise the reawakening that the city and region are currently experiencing. So the building itself became an experiment in many respects – structurally, technically, ecologically and in terms of craftsmanship – challenging a building industry that is already undergoing major changes in the transition to digitalisation.

Finally, the new Experimenta building stands in a long tradition of spiral-shaped buildings, that stretches from antiquity to modernity and contemporary times. From Jacob's Ladder to the Guggenheim Museum via the Tower of Babel, this particular spatial concept has been interpreted in various ways. Its latest transformation into a science centre expands the idea of metaphorical ascent in a striking and innovative way. Florian Heilmeyer's essay traces the spiral in architectural history and explains the cultural roots and associations that led to the new Experimenta building. LH MS

Heilbronn

The History of
a European City

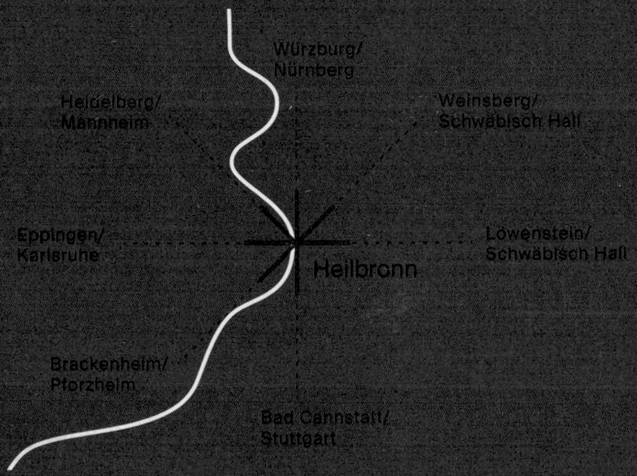

Würzburg/
Nürnberg

Heidelberg/
Mannheim

Weinsberg/
Schwäbisch Hall

Eppingen/
Karlsruhe

Löwenstein/
Schwäbisch Hall

Heilbronn

Brackenheim/
Pforzheim

Bad Cannstatt/
Stuttgart

Crossroads

Traces of human settlements have existed in the Heilbronn basin for around 30,000 years. A shallow ford makes the Nikros, the 'wild, turbulent river', passable, which meant that eight regional and supra-regional trade routes converged here.

Roman legions secured the strategically important crossing with a fort near today's Böckingen and as early as the 12th or 13th century a fixed bridge was installed. Like a spider weaving a web, Heilbronn developed a lively network and became a hub of commercial activity as a market, trading centre and river port.

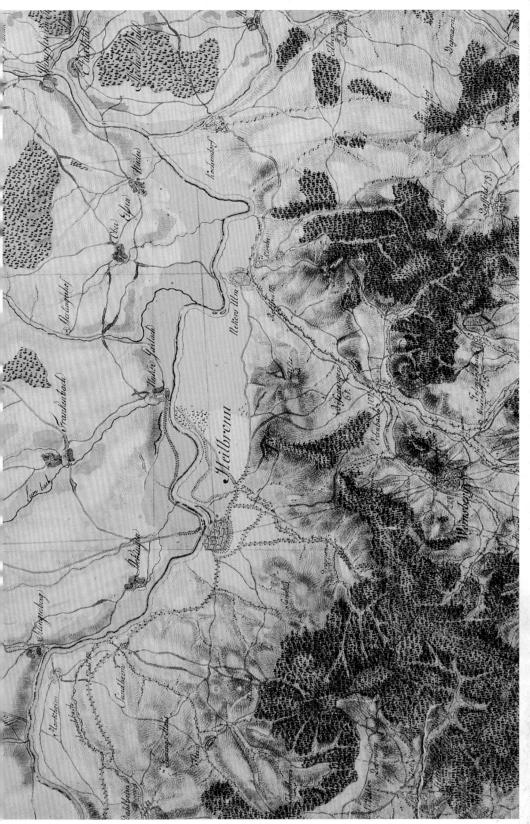

Detail from the Schmitt map of South-West Germany, 1797

5

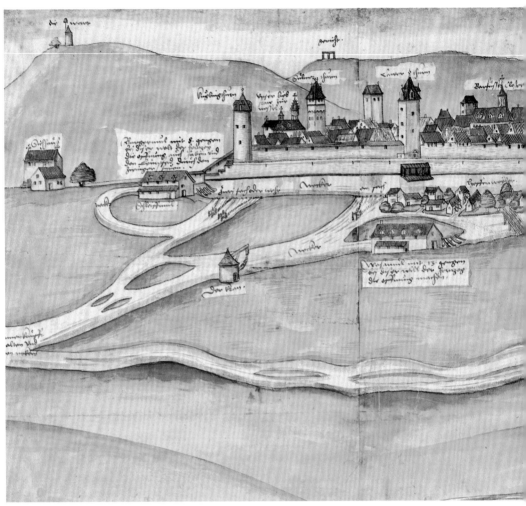

Earliest extant view of Heilbronn, as seen from the west, c. 1554

Hydropower and
the Neckar privilege

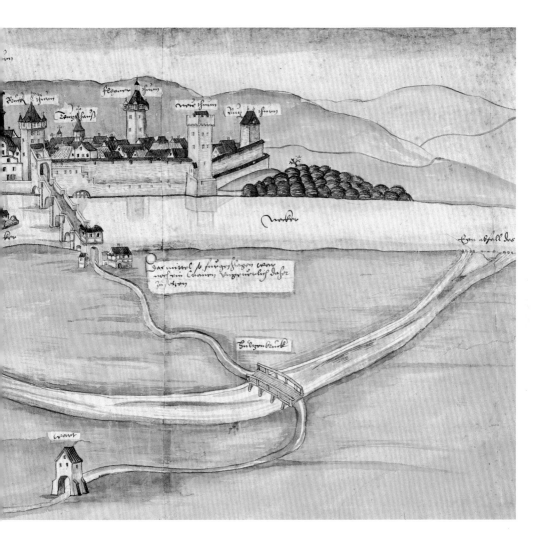

Time and again the river overflowed its banks, flooding parts of the Heilbronn basin, a problem that the city addressed by building artificial islands, canals and weirs in a bid to control the river. The first mills were built on the islands and along the banks, using the water as a source of power. These interventions led to repeated conflicts with the other riparian settlements up- and downstream.

When the weirs caused the river to overflow its banks and flood the estates of the Teutonic Order, the dispute came before Emperor Ludwig. In 1333 he granted the people of Heilbronn the so-called 'Neckar Privilege', the official right to change the course of the river 'at will'. This became the cornerstone of Heilbronn's prosperity.

Little Venice

The weirs presented an insurmountable obstacle for river navigation as every ship had to unload and reload its cargo. Heilbronn made money by levying a 'stacking tariff' and the haulage business flourished.

The first crane that we know of was erected in 1514 by the architect and stonemason Hans Schweiner on the riverbank outside the city gates, making the transhipment of goods even faster. Heilbronn's most powerful neighbour, Duke Christoph of Württemberg, complained to the emperor about the Neckar privilege: he called Heilbronn a 'little Venice', intent on 'taking over all matters pertaining to trade and commerce'. For centuries the city refused to remove the weirs and the Neckar remained impassable until the opening of the Wilhelm Canal in 1821.

Detail of a view of the city from 1643 showing the crane built by Hans Schweiner in 1513/14

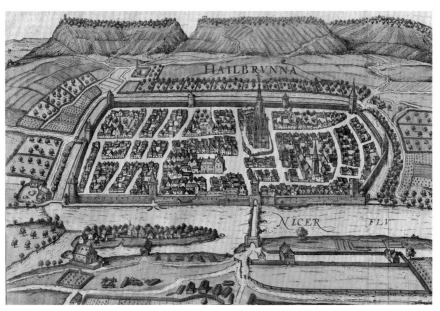

Idealised view of the fortified city as seen from the west, 1617

View of the Hefenweiler from the south, 1861

Liverpool in Württemberg

Historic centre north of Lohtorstrasse, with the Rauch and Schaeuffelen paper factories in the background, c.1895.

The industrialisation of Heilbronn was likewise initiated on the river islands. In the early 19th century, ever larger machines were used in the paper mills, enabling increasingly efficient production. Other industries followed and by 1832 Heilbronn had become the city with the most factories in the Kingdom of Württemberg. Because of its many smokestacks, Heilbronn was no longer spoken of as 'Little Venice' but was known instead as 'the Swabian Liverpool'.

Up to 55 waterwheels were in operation in the islands' mill district, which became more and more densely built. The factory owners who lived there included the Rauch, Schaeuffelen, Münzing and Knorr families. The construction of the Wilhelm Canal in 1821 offered river shipping a new way that avoided the mill weirs – although by this time the stacking tariff had become obsolete, as Heilbronn had fallen to Württemberg in 1802.

The Wilhelm Canal, seen from the north with a view of the historic city centre, c.1850

Growth

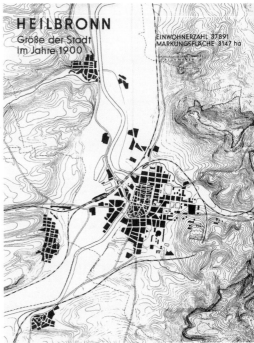

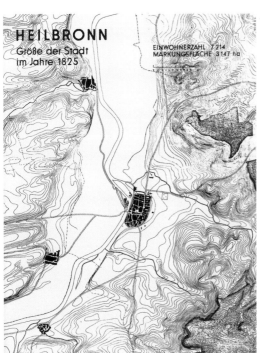

Maps showing the city's expansion between 1825 and 1900 – from a pamphlet published by the city planning office, 1965

In the 19th century, the population of Heilbronn increased sixfold, from 5,700 inhabitants in 1803 to 37,900 in 1900.

The city gates and walls were taken down and new suburbs were built west of the Neckar. At the beginning of the 20th century about a quarter of Heilbronn's inhabitants were factory workers.

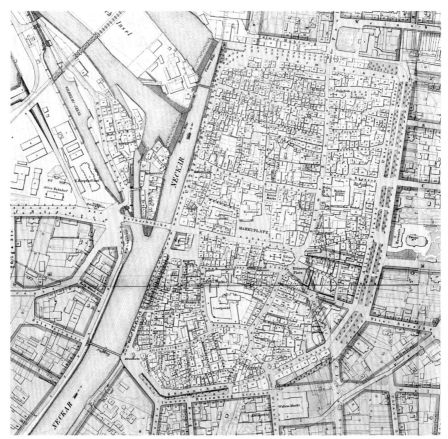

Plan for the city of Heilbronn, 1879

Leap across the Neckar

In 1848 the railway station was constructed next to the Wilhelm Canal in the western suburbs. Reinhard Baumeister's general urban development plan of 1873 envisaged Kaiserstrasse as a magnificent east-west axis connecting the historic centre and the suburbs. By the time the industrial trade fair took place in 1897, the plan had largely been implemented. Even though the old town remained the centre, the regional and supra-regional connections and the constantly expanding western suburbs steadily gained in importance.

The oil baron's castle

View of the Neckar islands from the south, 1921

In 1896 the brothers Karl and Louis Hagenbucher bought the Brückenmühle mill on the Neckar's Kraneninsel (Crane Island). Their company quickly grew to become one of the largest oil producers in the German Empire. From the Neckar Bridge, the increasingly dense grouping of buildings and the industrial activity on the Hefenweiler and Kraneninsel islands were clearly visible. Although 'only' cooking oil was produced there, people spoke, half reverently and half in jest, of the 'oil baron's castle'.

The company prospered and soon needed a new warehouse for the heavy oil seeds. By 1936 an extremely robust and modern seven-storey building had been constructed. Designed by Hermann Wahl, it had a reinforced concrete skeleton with a dark brick façade and was known as the Hagenbucher.

Even on the third floor, it was capable of storing up to three tonnes per square metre. One unintended side effect of such a robust construction was that during the bombardments of the Second World War the cellars of the warehouse could be deployed as an air-raid shelter.

The Hagenbucher

The Hagenbucher company's new oilseed warehouse, 1937

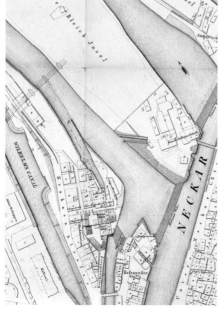

Kraneninsel and Hefenweiler in an extract from the building records for Brückenmühlweg 6, printed in 1850, drawings from 1883

The Hagenbucher warehouse under construction, 1936

Aerial photograph of the city centre taken from a Zeppelin, 1930

17

The town hall in ruins, 1945

At the end of the war Heilbronn lay in ruins. The old town was deemed to have been totally destroyed, with the devastation affecting 57 per cent of the city as a whole.

All five bridges across the Neckar had been blown up by the retreating Wehrmacht and the mill district including the oil baron's castle on the Neckar islands had also been reduced to rubble. Only the Hagenbucher warehouse emerged intact.

Destruction

Aerial image of the historic centre, 1945. View from the west, with Kraneninsel and Hefenweiler in the foreground.

Aerial image of the historic centre in May 1957. View from the south-west.

The miracle of Heilbronn

Following the clearance of debris, an astonishingly rapid process of reconstruction began. Revised zoning of the land available for construction enabled fundamental changes to be made to the city's historical structure as it was being rebuilt: the new version of the formerly dense old town was significantly more spacious and amenable to vehicles.

Rebuilt town hall with annex, 1962

Aerial view of the former Mühlenviertel, 1957

The last remains of the industrial buildings on the Neckar islands were destroyed and the old waterways filled in. In the old mill district only the Hagenbucher warehouse remained, having survived the bombing almost unscathed. As the demolition of such a sturdy building would have been too expensive, it remained standing, even though the company that had given it its name had ceased to exist.

In 1959 the Hagenbucher came into municipal ownership and the warehouse was rented out for storage. On the Hefenweiler, the Insel Hotel was built between 1952 and 1959 beside the new Neckar Bridge. It was planned by Kurt Marohn, who also designed the Harmonie concert hall in the late fifties and the Kilian shopping arcade in the late sixties and consequently became the most important architect in post-war Heilbronn.

Reconstruction and transformation

The era of the automobile had started back in the 1920s. But it was only in the post-war era with the reconstruction of the historic centre that Heilbronn was able to become thoroughly oriented towards the automobile – and its ever-increasing population of car owners – with wide, generously proportioned main streets and dedicated pedestrian zones. The Neckar was spanned by slender reinforced concrete bridges and the motorway network was extended to Mannheim, Würzburg and Nuremberg.

Of the Neckar islands, only the Hefenweiler and the Kraneninsel remained, while the Bleichinseln were ultimately integrated into the riverbank using rubble infill. The area known as Hospitalgrün was set to become the beginning of a coherent urban park that would include the islands and run along the banks of the river; the implementation of these plans, however, would get bogged down for decades to come.

During reconstruction, Fleiner Strasse in the historic centre becomes a street for commerce and cars, in this photograph from 1959. In the background, we can see the Merkur department store designed by Egon Eiermann.

Car city

Traffic now flows where the river used to run: Mannheimer Strasse lies above a former arm of the River Neckar that has been filled with debris from the old town, with the 'Hospitalgrün' on the left, 1957.

New building for Reifen-Friedle in Neckarsulmer Strasse, 1957

High-rise building for the *Heilbronner Stimme* from 1957

High-rises

iew over the historic centre and the Hafenmarkt tower towards the 14-storey Shoppinghaus building from 1971

Along the new, wide traffic corridors, high-rise buildings such as the City Hotel, the Shoppinghaus, the *Heilbronner Stimme* and the Wollhauszentrum sprang up, with these giants effectively establishing themselves as familiar figures in the cityscape.

The influx of cars caused the various cities in the Heilbronn basin to merge more and more into one another. The river valley was transformed into an interconnected agglomeration with blurred dividing lines.

Traffic jam in Fleiner Strasse, 1970

A scrambled egg

If one goes along with the metaphor conceived by the great British architect Cedric Price, then this marked the culmination of Heilbronn's successful development from a hard-boiled egg (a city with a hard border – defined, for example, by historical city walls) via a fried egg (a city with a clearly recognisable historical centre and fluidly distributed periphery) to a scrambled egg (a city with many dispersed centres and fuzzy boundaries).

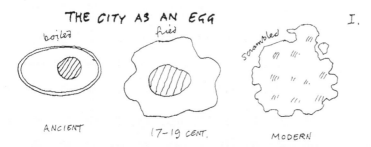

Cedric Price, *The City as an Egg*, c. 2001

New urban and industrial landscapes

View across Neckargartach Bridge and the heat and power plant towards Neckarsulm in the north, 1967

Besides the factories that processed chemical, paper and foodstuffs, it was primarily the metals and electrical industries in the Heilbronn basin that gained in importance, with many of these companies supplying southern Germany's ever-expanding automotive industry.

Following the incorporation of some further communities, Heilbronn's population passed the 100,000 mark for the first time in 1970 and by 2020 it had grown to over 125,000.

Since the 1950s, the city had sought to establish a park on the remaining islands in the river and along its banks. The plans, however, had gone little further than feasibility studies until the 1990s, when new footbridges were built that turned the islands into crossing points, effectively making them part of the city centre. The Hagenbucher warehouse now became incorporated into the plan for an urban park, and a municipal museum was due to move in, although no agreement was reached on either financing or programming.

Art in the warehouse

Neue Kunst im Hagenbucher exhibition, 1993

Blue-green Heilbronn

By the turn of the millennium, it had become clear that the industries around Heilbronn – and especially the automotive industry – needed to reinvent themselves. The city had begun at an early stage to adapt its infrastructures to the vision of a sustainable Heilbronn with green and blue axes of local recreation. In 1988 the nearby city of Karlsruhe had extended its light rail system to Heilbronn, and in 2013 Neckarsulm was connected in as well.

Back in 1985, as part of the Regional Garden Show, a section of the riverbank had been turned into Wertwiesen Park, and in 2019, as part of the BUGA National Garden Show, 40 hectares of a former industrial site between the Neckar Canal and the old arm of the river were redesigned as a park, including an ecologically sustainable residential quarter. This finally brought the new blue-green concept directly to the Kraneninsel and Hefenweiler islands.

ew of the National Garden Show (BUGA) and the new Neckarbogen residential area from the north-west, 2019

Tropical fruit

A. Lidl & Co, Sülmerstrasse 54, c.1905

A protagonist of some significance in this latest reinvention of Heilbronn is the entrepreneur Dieter Schwarz, who was born in Heilbronn in 1939. His father had joined A. Lidl & Co. Südfrüchtenhandlung, a chain of shops selling tropical fruits and other goods, which he developed into a food wholesaler.

By 1963 Schwarz had risen to become a partner in his father's business. Trading as the Handelshof discount store, Lidl & Schwarz KG opened its first self-service shop in Backnang in 1968. In 1984 Schwarz founded the Kaufland supermarket chain and by 2020 the Schwarz Group had become the largest retail concern in Europe (in terms of annual turnover).

The Dieter Schwarz Foundation was set up in November 1999, with the mission of establishing a framework of higher education and professional training in Schwarz's home region. This would enable each generation to discover the most appropriate solutions for the particular issues it needed to address. In his view, this was the only way that the city and region could hope to continually reinvent themselves in a successful manner.

The Bildungscampus (Educational Campus) Heilbronn opened in 2011 on 7 hectares of a former industrial site. All the new buildings were paid for by the foundation, which also provides funding to help run the university. In 2018 the Technical University of Munich (TUM) relocated part of its business administration faculty to the new campus and so Heilbronn could now legitimately call itself a university city. The foundation finances 20 professorships at the TUM, 13 of which must be located in Heilbronn. In 2021 the newspaper DIE ZEIT referred to this agreement as a 'coup in higher educational policy that is unprecedented in Germany'.

Continuous reinvention

The Heilbronn Educational Campus, initiated and financed by the Dieter Schwarz Foundation

Experimenta

The Hagenbucher warehouse: before (above) and after (below) conversion.

In 2004 the Dieter Schwarz Foundation took up the city's plans to establish a cultural institution in the Hagenbucher warehouse, two years later financing a feasibility study to investigate the conversion of the building into a science centre.

The foundation saw this as a key element in the upcoming educational campus with its focus on lifelong learning and its encouragement of children and adolescents to take a playful approach to complex questions from the realms of science and technology. The city and foundation shared the costs of the renovation work carried out by Studio Inges from Berlin and on 14 November 2009 Experimenta was inaugurated in the Hagenbucher building.

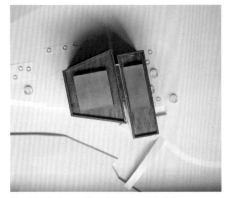

The joint between the old and new building can be clearly seen in the model.

New building

Before long 100,000 visitors a year were flocking to the Hagenbucher, so that the warehouse quite quickly became too small for the Science Centre. In 2013 the foundation announced that an extension would be built next to the converted warehouse on the Kraneninsel island, a highly symbolic location that is a focal point for Heilbronn's narratives of continuous reinvention spanning more than 1,200 years of the city's history. Accordingly, the new building became both a symbol and an instrument of Heilbronn's latest incarnation and its future processes of reinvention. In 2013 Sauerbruch Hutton's concept for the new building convinced the jury of the international architectural competition and the office was commissioned to implement their design.

Experimenta

Harbinger of the
Knowledge Society

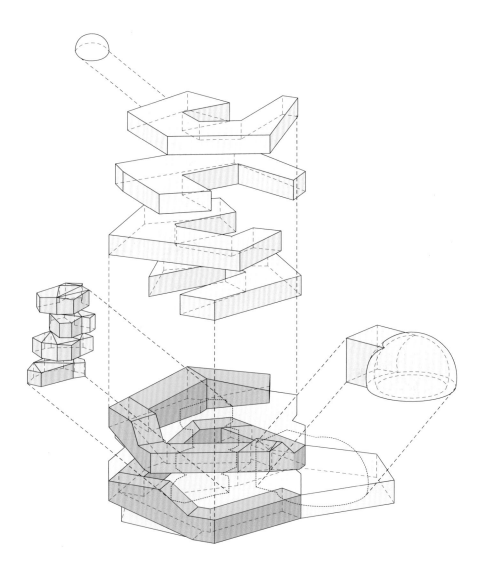

New buildings are often expected to be inconspicuous: they should accommodate and blend in with their surroundings, in some cases so much so that the new merges with the old and can barely be recognised as such.

In view of the great longing for lost buildings to be reconstructed, as has been the vogue in recent decades, one can almost detect a certain neophobia in Germany, a fear, that is, of anything new. People prefer to stick with what they already know. So for a building to be charged, right from the start, with symbolising a new departure is something of an exception – and yet this was what both the city and the client explicitly wanted for the extension to Experimenta. The architectural competition in 2013 called for an emblematic building that would symbolise the spirit of curiosity and the playful urge to explore that which this science centre was intended to communicate. In addition to this, it was to be a contemporary 'eye-catcher', which would attract both national and international attention.

A spiral space rooted in the city

The exposed location on the Kraneninsel island, which sits opposite the historic centre of Heilbronn and is surrounded on three sides by the water of the old arm of the Neckar, made the site an obvious choice for the development of such an emblematic building. Footpaths and bikeways traversed the site from all directions leading to the old Hagenbucher warehouse, where the existing part of Experimenta was already housed. Just as Heilbronn itself originated at such a crossroads, Experimenta was now establishing itself at a place that had become a small sub-centre in the heart of the city – albeit one that had been largely disregarded in the past.

Based on this rather particular situation, Sauerbruch Hutton developed a design that brings focus to the dynamics of the junction and weaves the routes together, like threads twined to create a strong rope. This rationale led to the idea of an upward spiral movement, a strong gesture that became the central motif of the new Experimenta. The resulting helical space develops clearly out of its location but at the same time is powerfully and unmistakably new. It is as if the new building were to immediately take root, becoming an inextricable part of the local fabric and – via the intersecting paths that reach out like tentacles – of the entire city.

This spiral-shaped space begins as a promenade even outside the entrance door: between the old and new, the public terrain becomes a common forecourt for both buildings. Through floor-to-ceiling glazing, both foyers open onto an in-between exterior space. This creates a strong connection – stronger even than the underground passageway that actually connects the two buildings. On entering the new Experimenta, visitors follow a route that leads towards the left through the foyer, past the ticket and information counters, lifts and museum shop to the first escalator.

In the vortex

This is where the ascent into the helical space starts, with the route orbiting the core of the building: the escalators are not centrally located as they would be in, say, a department store but instead follow the contours of the clear glass façades as they wind up the perimeter of the structure. At every level, visitors are welcomed by a large, clearly arranged foyer. The varying rotations of the floors mean that each foyer opens up in a different direction. On the first floor, the view is directed north-west over the Kraneninsel island – the grounds of the BUGA Federal Garden Show can just be glimpsed behind the trees along the river. On the second floor the view shifts to a north-easterly orientation, looking out over the Bollwerk Tower, the skating rink and the water park, with the university campus visible beyond. In the background there is a view of the Wartberg mountain, whose vineyards occupy the limit of what can be seen. Arriving on the third floor, the massive Hagenbucher warehouse blocks the main aspect, but to the left the view extends far out over the river and across the roofs of the old town. The tower of St Kilian's Church and the high-rise buildings of the Heilbronner Stimme and the Wollhaus provide orientation, with the view behind them reaching all the way to the Heilbronn Hills. On the fourth floor, the perspective opens up to the north again, but in contrast to the first floor the panorama now extends out above the trees, so that one can see the railway station to the left and the BUGA grounds straight ahead, with the Heilbronn basin in the distance stretching towards

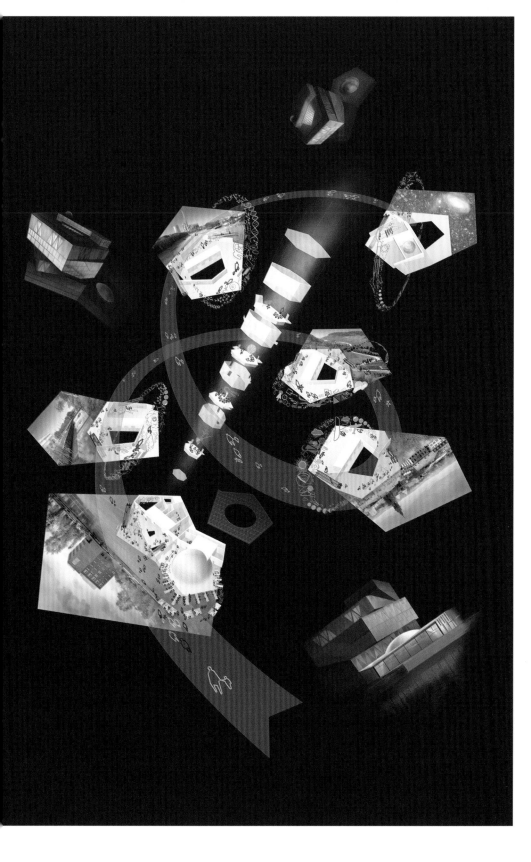

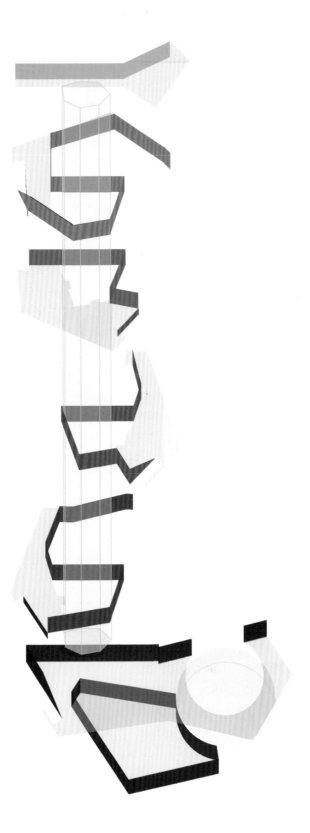

46

Neckarsulm. One last escalator leads us to the top floor, to the small stage of the experimental theatre, which is completely introverted, and – for maximum contrast – to the large roof terrace, which offers an almost complete panorama of 360 degrees. This is interrupted only by the small dome of the observatory, a comparatively compact space at the end of this 'spiral of knowledge' that directs our view through two telescopes to the final frontiers of the human imagination: outer space.

The dynamic of taking visitors upwards through a spirally formed building has a number of famous precedents in architecture, the most prominent of which is Frank Lloyd Wright's Guggenheim Museum in New York. To be sure, in Heilbronn the basic layout of the spiral-shaped promenade is not a contrivance but a practical piece of spatial organisation and symbolic expression all in one: en route the generous panoramic foyers are at the same time lobbies for the themed exhibitions, where the visitors inevitably meet each other when going up or down. As both entrances and exits are easy to hold in one's field of vision, this is where groups naturally gather before or after visiting an exhibition. At the same time, the respective views of the foyers open up more and more, the higher they ascend the 'path of knowledge'. The accumulation of information expands our horizons and culminates in the view from the roof terrace, which stretches across the whole region and, via the observatory, ultimately extends into the depths of the universe.

The foyers: Vistas and points of view

Although the view may be different on the various floors, the organisation of the set of spaces on each of the four levels always remains the same: the respective foyer begins and ends with an escalator and, in between, the space opens up like a belvedere, where visitors can linger and enjoy the various panoramas as they look out over Heilbronn. These foyers provide a moment of pause – in the best sense: they can be used as spontaneous or planned meeting places or for a variety of informal events. There are also interactive stations where one can carry out an individual evaluation of the section of the exhibition one has just visited and the effect it has achieved.

The foyers are also clearly distinct from one another by virtue of their expansive rear walls, which are painted in shades of red with a different tonality on every floor, from the basement up to the roof terrace. The spectrum ranges from the dark-red tones of ferrous earth via the familiar vermilion hues of flora and fauna and a pinkish orange to tangerine on the uppermost floor: this is only a slight chromatic step away from the fiery swirls on the surface of the sun that can be seen through the telescopes on the roof terrace. Integrated into these coloured rear walls are two wide doorways that serve as entrance and exit for the variously themed exhibition areas. Between these lies the vertical axis of the building, around which the spiral space twists up like a vortex. This axis is empha- sised by an atrium that stretches up the entire height of the building and allows visitors to look both up and down – to the floors that lie ahead of them and to those they have already traversed. In the centre of this atrium a kind of cocoon is suspended that consists of four crystalline, irregularly shaped and fully glazed studios, one on each floor. These are reached via short bridge connections that also act as supports. This cocoon-like stack hovers above the ground floor, where its glowing underside illuminates the space of the foyer. From below, visitors can look upwards through the gap around the cocoon and so grasp the entire height of the building in a single glance.

The cocoon contains the so-called Creative Studios, in which young visitors have the opportunity to conduct small experiments in order to apply what they have learned or experienced in the exhibitions. This consolidates the knowledge they have gained and in each case allows them to construct for themselves a souvenir of their visit.

Stacked theatre spaces

On each floor the themed exhibitions are arranged in U-shaped formations around the atrium. If one were to apply the metaphor of the building as a 'mountain of knowledge' to be scaled, then the themed exhibitions would be like tempting caves: on entering these, visitors first leave the light-flooded foyers to arrive in dark reception areas where the respective themes are introduced. Behind these, some 800 square metres of (variously designed) exhibition areas

open up with some 60 to 70 interactive stations. To enable whatever the desired mise en scène might be for each particular exhibit, these parts of the building have remained almost completely closed to the outside: they are basically theatrical spaces – contained, robust and equipped with versatile technological equipment – that allow for every imaginable form of spatial presentation. The façades therefore needed to remain largely opaque to enable the inner surfaces of the exterior walls to be deployed from the inside. Every now and then sizeable expanses of translucent frosted glazing let in subdued daylight (where visitors can catch glimpses of the outside world) – but even these can be entirely closed.

A comprehensive visit to Experimenta can easily take a whole day, so it is appropriate that the foyer areas between the stimulating exhibitions offer space for one to catch one's breath, chat, gather one's thoughts or even enjoy a small snack. The building's basic organisation means that visitors are constantly alternating between close-up and distant views – between the extroverted gaze outside and the introverted focus on the various phenomena being presented, some of which can only be seen with the microscope – that actually constitute and give coherence to the reality outside the window. In other words, the building itself, as an architectural 'parkour', mediates between the panoramic expanse and the microscopic and so helps to establish the connection between inside and outside, between large-scale and small-scale, between macro and micro. In addition to this, the continuous alternation between the artificial light that illuminates the staging of various natural and scientific phenomena and the bright daylight that floods the foyers helps visitors to maintain their concentration and receptiveness.

The architects Matthias Sauerbruch and Louisa Hutton refer to their new building as a 'cathedral of learning': it should be 'a tool, a stage and a sculpture all at the same time', a 'monument to curiosity'. It is above all the utility of the balanced spatial structure that ensures that the architecture of Experimenta never slides into formalism. It was not the intention to create either a vain work of art or an overly symbolic monument. Although the spiral space can happily be read as a symbol or emblem, it functions first and foremost as a practical device for providing pleasurable and easy access to a series of well-equipped, stacked workshop and exhibition spaces that are ready to be set up for Experimenta's ever-changing interactive displays.

This is precisely the impression that the new building projects towards the outside as well. Concerning both form and materiality, the new structure could hardly exhibit a more different architectural language than the older one: it is unmistakably a contemporary intervention made of steel and glass with façades that present a sense of expansive connection with, and openness to, the surroundings. As such, it is anything but nostalgic. Yet, at the same time, the new building does not supplant the old one, even though it is much larger and also occupies a more prominent, eye-catching location on the bend in the river. In fact, it radiates the kind of robustness one finds in the old warehouse: it is clear that they are closely related – both sturdy utilitarian buildings – one almost 100 years older than the other.

Yet, even after the conversion and extension by Studio Inges, the power of the older building's brick façades gives it the air of a raw block that has been roughly hewn out of a larger whole. By contrast, the new building appears like an oversized version of Rubik's famous cube, whose offset levels could perhaps be aligned with a few deft movements of the hand if we only possessed the stature and strength to twist it. The respectful distance between these two 'brothers' is just as important as the discretion between their respective material and colour treatments. In contrast to other buildings by Sauerbruch Hutton, no strongly hued spectrum comes to the fore. On the contrary, the black, pale bluish-grey and white tones of the new building make it seem almost monochrome by day: the façades of the foyers appearing as a series of large, dark, rectangular windows, while the exterior walls fronting the exhibition areas are clad with white glass panes, which reflect the zigzag of the steel framework behind. In between, delicate pale blue-grey areas shimmer translucently. Although the new building may represent the opposite of its older counterpart, the two structures do actually come close to one another in terms of their economy of means. It is precisely this restraint that underlines the size and powerful angular presence of both buildings, which, despite being such opposites on their shared island, look like what they are: a complementary pair. The two distinctive structures unite to become

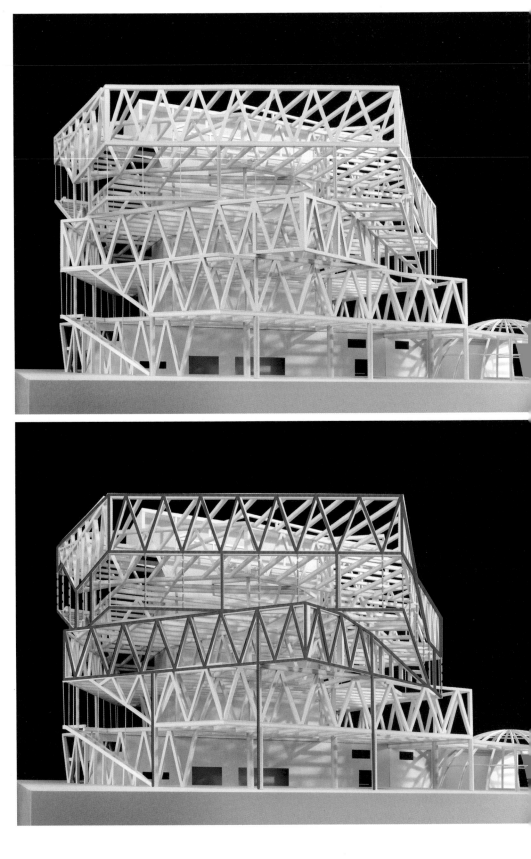

a single ensemble, in which the addition of the new building helps to bring out the monumental and sculptural qualities of the existing warehouse even more clearly. A survivor from a bygone era, the Hagenbucher warehouse had become a mysterious relic, a strangely large and bulky volume with an inexplicably trapezoidal ground plan that lacked any point of reference. This building can only be understood as a fragment of the former industrial landscape of the Neckar islands, a monument to *temps perdu*. The new Experimenta has given the warehouse a fresh point of reference that restores a sense of equilibrium.

Only at dusk and at night does the impression change. Then the light inside brings both depth and colour to the new building: the eye reaches deep into the foyers with their five differing shades of red on their rear walls, so these deep, colourful spaces suddenly become an integral part of the external experience of the architecture. At the same time, small figures become visible as they circulate through the foyers and float up and down the escalators: the visitors' movement becomes part of the image, like a procession on a modern, well-lit secular Calvary. As the new Experimenta comes to life in this way at night, it assumes a quality of transparency that contrasts with the solidity – and reticence – of the old building. The latter keeps to itself whatever its visitors get up to inside, while the narrow glass seam connecting it to the annex picks up on the motif of transparency.

The seven super-columns

The spiral-shaped space with its various foyer areas offset against each other had been adopted as an architectural leitmotif relatively early on in the design process. However, the consequence of this quite fundamental design decision introduced a considerable challenge with regard to the development of an appropriate structural system. The changing layout of each floor and the rotation of the spaces relative to one another required a complex structural framework, which was developed by the architects in close cooperation with the engineers at schlaich bergermann partner and the team at Advanced Building Technologies. Together, they created a three-dimensional digital model that mirrored the entire building. This was then parametrically modelled, calculated, optimised and, in the end, materialised using production plans drawn up in close collaboration with the various fabricators and manufacturers. This joint work on a digital model, as a virtual space in which all the information about a building can be collected is still a relatively new method in the fields of architectecture and construction that has only slowly begun to gain acceptance in practice during the last decade. It was through the use of this digital model that the architects – in particular Peter Apel and Andrew Kiel – and engineers, under the direction of Michael Werwigk, developed what was ultimately an astonishingly simple and clearly articulated structural system. The form of the building does not follow function alone but was designed to enable the creation of useful and dramatic spaces – while at the same time taking a certain delight in the complex balance of forces.

The building is divided into two structural areas. A relatively small core made of reinforced concrete that accommodates the lifts and ancillary and technical rooms provides the horizontal bracing for the entire structure. Owing to the generous internal height of the exhibition spaces, the core is able to accommodate two storeys, with concealed mezzanine floors providing additional technical rooms. However, those areas of the building that comprise the entire upward-spiralling space are supported by just seven composite columns. One can describe these without exaggeration as super-columns: steel tubes with a diameter of 70 centimetres filled with reinforced concrete. They support storey-high steel trusses that carry the loads of the exhibition areas. These trusses either sit on top of each other or cantilever up to the next super-column without deformation. The spiralling or helical space itself – that is, the series of foyers together with the escalators that bind them – running in between these floors is actually supported by very slender columns that are suspended from the respective steel truss above. In consequence, the façades of the spiralling space are almost completely free of load-bearing supports and so remain totally transparent. This dual structural system is easily recognisable from the outside: the façades around the exhibition areas are mostly opaque and display the zigzag of the steel trusses in their cladding, while the generous, glazed foyers can instantly be grasped

by virtue of the rectangular formats of their large, transparent panes. Thanks to the structural system, the glass façades of the foyers – which do not have to bear any load except their own – could be fitted with quite spectacular windowpanes, the largest measuring some 5 by 3 metres. Meanwhile, the seven supercolumns, which one encounters here and there as one traverses the foyers, have not been played as main elements in the design but appear as somewhat unsung elements of inconspicuous shape and colour that quietly perform their service.

The digital model was also available to all the other planning specialists, who could use it to continuously add and update their information, so that the design of the building could be constantly checked for any potential problems and optimised. In addition, this digital simulacrum of the building could be put through all kinds of stress tests, like an aircraft in a flight simulator. In this way, the stability under extreme wind or snow loads could be simulated and the structure perfected accordingly. At Experimenta, this was all the more important because the observatory on the roof has telescopes that are extremely sensitive to vibrations. In order for this particular equipment to function, the steel structure had to be redesigned so as to be particularly robust and able to withstand the transmission of vibrations – for example, even from the movements of visitors.

Computing the design for the basement areas was similarly demanding: here one finds not only the technical spaces for building services, cloakrooms and a direct tunnel connection to the old building, but also a 650-square-metre hall with a height of up to 8 metres. This space is for special exhibitions and at the same time allows for the gathering of large groups of school children. An adjacent hall, up to 10 metres high, constitutes the so-called Science Dome – a special theatre in which scientific shows can be combined in a demonstration with the experience of a planetarium. To make this possible, the rows of seating for 150 visitors can be rotated 180 degrees independently of the theatre's outer shell. To start with, the audience faces the stage but once the seating has rotated, their view is directed towards a domed ceiling, on which a planetarium provided by Zeiss projects the night sky. This enormous basement lies in a waterproof, reinforced and prestressed concrete construction, which also bears the loads of the building above. Since this entire volume is submerged in water, it had to be made watertight in all the external areas and secured against uplift with tie rods.

The various systems of the building's supporting structure thus not only provide the ideal static system to convey the building's architectural intent but are also a perfected example – by any measure – of the joy of knowledge and research that is playfully communicated by Experimenta to visitors of all ages.

The building as an experiment and harbinger of change

Clearly, the new Experimenta in Heilbronn is itself an experiment in that it explores new routes in its spatial and structural concept and at the same time plays a pioneering role in its design. As a matter of fact, this also applies to questions of sustainability. A building made of glass, steel and concrete is generally not considered a good model in this respect. Here, however, the integrated planning process made it possible to consider aspects of sustainability right from the start of the design process and to verify them continuously at all levels. The construction was planned in such a way that almost all the materials and elements of construction can be separated and either reused or recycled with very little loss should the structure be subsequently adapted or even dismantled. Since the steel construction can be completely disassembled, the building is not the end user of the material but acts as a temporary store, a material resource for the future. The panoramic panes of the glass façade were developed in close cooperation with specialist planners and manufacturers to allow digital printing and a special coating to achieve an optimum balance between transparency, daylight penetration and the lowest possible heat gain or loss. These moves to achieve reductions in energy demand are augmented by an interior climate concept that operates with low heating and high cooling temperatures: the combination of activated building components, gravity cooling and heat recovery systems enables the interior of Experimenta to be climate controlled without producing draughts or noise emissions, creating a very comfortable environment for visitors and staff alike. Heat pumps ensure that 75 per cent of the total thermal demand is harvested from groundwater, while the geothermally sourced energy caters for 100 per cent of the building's cooling needs. The reduction in cooling load alone saves some 200 tonnes of CO_2 emissions annually compared to conventional cooling methods. As a result, the new building was able to achieve the Platinum Label, the highest-level certification of the German Sustainable Building Council (DGNB) – and, after completion, the DGNB's new Diamond classification, which has only very rarely been awarded to date: this rating is assigned by a jury to buildings in which both passive and active elements of sustainable building are combined with excellent design and high architectural quality.

The courage to innovate has been rewarded in Heilbronn: an unusual piece of architecture fulfils its mission with a lack of pretension in its offer of a structure that meets the needs of Experimenta and provides a robust and at the same time ludic and enjoyable framework for its constantly changing experimental set-ups. The new building appears to be relaxed about its highly symbolic presence. Experimenta's mission is to turn children into researchers and to arouse curiosity in all walks of society – curiosity about new findings, about new knowledge and about innovation. Science is not a panacea in this respect and, as a science centre, Experimenta is not interested in simply reproducing knowledge that has already been established. Instead, it aims to encourage people to keep asking questions themselves and to look for different, innovative solutions. For it is the delight in curiosity and knowledge that has enabled Heilbronn and the local region to advance, just as it has spurred the evolution of humanity as a whole throughout the history of our species, which dates back some 100,000 years. The new Experimenta building is both a symbol of this curiosity and a monument to it – a tool for the constantly recurring, necessary and, above all, joyful reinvention of the city and the surrounding region. It is difficult to imagine, one might argue, that anything better could have happened to Heilbronn than the arrival of this new 'urban crown', which has developed in such a relatable way from the logic of its remit, its urban context and the city's history.

Basement floor

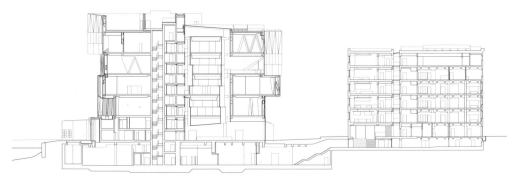

Section A

Ground floor

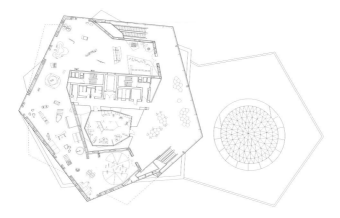

Second floor

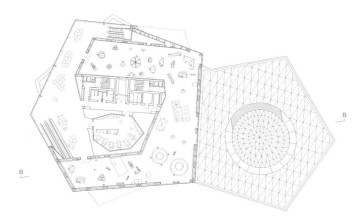

First floor

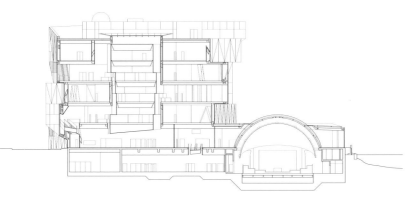

Section B

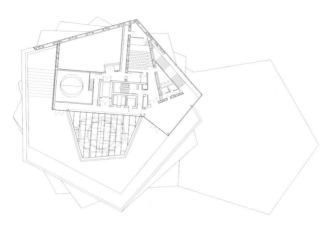

Fifth floor

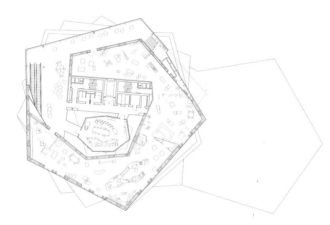

Fourth floor

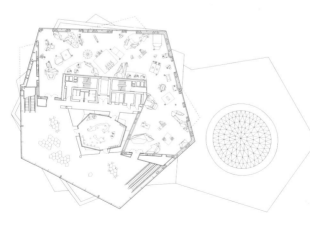

Third floor

66

Flights of Knowledge

The Human Longing to Ascend: A Short Cultural History

The *Ladder of Divine Ascent,* a 12th-century
icon from St Catherine's Monastery on
Mount Sinai. It shows monks who, headed
by John Climacus, are being led up a
ladder of virtue to God, beset by all manner
of temptation.

Human-built ascents to the realms of the divine:
the Acropolis in Athens (above left); the
reconstructed Ziggurat of Ur (below); and Temple I
in the Mayan city of Tikal (right)

Up above us the Gods, the Light

Ever since mankind first contemplated the divine, the world has been clearly divided: Good is to be found above, Evil below, and humankind wanders the world somewhere in between. This orientation system applies to all human cultures of which we have found traces, and they share another common feature: the route to the divine has always been imagined as an ascent. Whether one thinks of the ziggurats in Mesopotamia, the stepped temples of the Mayas and Aztecs in Latin and South America, the high altars of the Pharaohs in Egypt or the mountain shrines of Greek antiquity, Buddhism or Taoism, all of these bear witness (in stone) to the same fundamental world order: if you want to approach the gods, you have to go up into the heavens, towards the light.

The paths taken to fulfil this ambition were many and various. These staged ascents – which were both impressive and arduous – were either reserved for festive processions on certain days of the year or were solely the prerogative of the holy: the priests and temple custodians. Some stepped pyramids in Central America were so steep that researchers have wondered whether people at the time were able to climb them at all, or whether the top plateaus were deliberately staged in such a way as to be inaccessible. The Temple of Heaven in Beijing, the *Tiantan*, for example, comprises three circular platforms that are accessed by four stairways, one from each of the cardinal directions, with the ascent becoming steeper and more difficult from platform to platform. Here in the spring the emperor, as the Son of Heaven, would request a good harvest; which particular members of the court were entitled to stand on which particular platform was probably a symbolic reflection of their position and prestige.

By the same token, many pilgrimage routes end at a high point – either on a natural plateau or, if this is not possible, an artificial one. Some pilgrims move through this last stage on their knees or even on their bellies. Here, the artificial hardship of the ascent is an integral part of the visit to the sanctuary. The climb is part of the ritual, as a period of consciously protracted humility, of inner contemplation, of gradual purification or of cathartic agony.

Of straight and spiral ascents

Even in the earliest surviving ritually staged ascents, there are two fundamentally different categories: the route that leads straight up

– in which pilgrims can always keep their eyes on their distant destination – or the winding, serpentine climb. The Acropolis in Athens offers a comparatively comfortable ascent, which is equally possible for the elderly and infirm, for carts and for families with children. In addition, a serpentine path provides an opportunity not only for contemplation but also for additional *mise en scène* – as was the case in the Christian calvaries that were subsequently established with stations from Christ's Way of the Cross. While the serpentine path promises slow, inner contemplation, a gradual, meditative withdrawal from earthly matters, the straight, steep route delivers immediate devotional agony.

Spiral staircases were early inventions of mankind. However, for centuries they have been used mainly as secondary connections when space was limited or as delivery routes. Some ziggurats have serpentine ramps and spiral staircases but these were probably used to allow access for heavy loads or ox carts, rather than as grand processional staircases. One of the oldest surviving spiral staircases, dating from 480 BCE and preserved in a Greek temple in Selinunte, Sicily, was surreptitiously carved into the rock at the rear of the buildings. In the Pharos of Alexandria, one of the tallest buildings of antiquity, scholars assume that there must have been spiral ramps inside the rectangular base that could be used to transport the huge quantities of material required. These ramps did not have any effect on the form of the building, however, and remained internal secrets.

The first exception to this is Trajan's Column in Rome, dating from AD 113. This 35-metre-tall triumphal monument is hollow: inside, 185 steps lead up to a viewing platform that gives onto the Forum. The staircase was open to the public and its ascending form is reflected in the famous spiralling frieze outside: the flight of steps has a visible architectural equivalent. Trajan's column became known throughout the ancient world, ensuring the spread of the spiral staircase in architecture as a symbol of prestige.

There is another structure that reverses this principle for the first time: the free-standing minaret of what was then the world's largest mosque was built in Samarra (present-day Iraq) in AD 852 as a massive 52-metre-high cone adjacent to the main building. Outside, a continuous ramp leads upwards as a spiral path around the building. This staged ascent, visible from afar, was a means to transport goods and workers during construction and was later used by the muezzin, and perhaps the Imam.

In the Lighthouse of Alexandria (above left), the spiral ramp remained hidden inside. The spiral frieze running up Trajan's Column in Rome (right) shows the path of the staircase inside. The 52-metre-high minaret next to the Great Mosque of Samarra (below) is a spiral ramp.

Changing depictions of Jacob's Ladder – in works
by Michael Willmann (1691, above left), Jacques
Réattu (1792, above right), Matthäus Merian
the Elder (1625, centre right) and William Blake
(1805, below right) and as a Bible illustration
(c.18th century, below left)

We know too little about this structure to say who was allowed to use this majestic route and whether there were any precedents for such a method of construction. Some suggest that Samarra may have been a smaller version of the Tower of Babel – whether it was modelled on the real thing or merely followed the narrative is irrelevant here. Or was it pure technical necessity that determined the overall form, as the materials could not otherwise be transported up to such a height? In any case, this minaret is the oldest extant building in which the spiral appears as an ordering device of, and design principle for, the architecture.

Over the following centuries, the spiral staircase increasingly asserted itself as the nobler and more ornate form vis-à-vis its straight-flight alternatives – a development that can be observed in parallel in both architecture and painting. It can be traced particularly vividly in paintings and drawings of two of the great themes of the Bible:

In Genesis, the first book of Moses,[1] we are told of an image that appears to Jacob in a dream as he is fleeing from Esau: in it, he sees a ladder (in Hebrew: *sullām*) leading from earth to heaven, into the light, to God. Angels are floating up and down, while the Lord stands above, announcing Jacob's entry into the promised land. Jacob awakens with his strength renewed and names the place Bet-El, the gateway to heaven. The Hebrew word sullām is ambiguous – it can be translated as a ladder but can also mean stairs or a ramp, so what exactly Jacob caught sight of as a connection between God and the human world is not clear. In pictorial representations prior to the 17th century, it was a very long, dead-straight ladder, which in many images is shown as a wobbly, swaying ladder of virtue, on which all kinds of devils and temptations endeavour to keep people from the precarious ascent. In Martin Luther's German translation of the Bible, it is also clearly 'Jacob's ladder', not 'Jacob's staircase' and certainly not 'Jacob's spiral staircase' or 'Jacob's ramp'.

So the representations remained uniform until modern times. Only then, with the awakening that accompanied Humanism and the Enlightenment, did the first depictions emerge in which Jacob sees a fixed staircase, which is then given a spiral form for the first time as a sign of its special, divine significance. This evolution from ladder to staircase – first straight, then curved – testifies to the escalation in cultural significance that was associated with the spiral staircase: this was nourished by increasingly

---

1 Gen. 28:10–13

elaborate examples and further fuelled by the rediscovery of pictorial perspective in the European Renaissance at almost the same time. Just as the construction of an elaborate spiral staircase demonstrates the expertise of its builder, the graphic construction of a spiral staircase meticulously projected into perspectival space is testament to the consummate artistry of the draughtsman.

Something else was also changing in the process: almost imperceptibly, with the growing influence of the Enlightenment and Humanism, it became increasingly unclear *where* this ascent was actually leading. Whereas early depictions had always featured a bearded figure of God the Father, in William Blake's 'Jacob's Dream', for example, which was painted in around 1800, the artist's skilfully rendered staircase turns towards an ill-defined light that could just as well represent divine illumination as enlightened knowledge – or does it simply reveal a dazzling natural phenomenon?

The second story also stems from Genesis: the Tower of Babel.[2] Nimrod commands his people to build a city with a tower whose top reaches into the sky. God hears of this, and fearing that soon nothing will seem out of reach to people, he confuses their language and scatters them across the globe. The tower remains unfinished. Like the story of Jacob's Ladder, the Tower of Babel has been depicted again and again throughout the history of Christian art, its image being continually reinvented in the process. In all early depictions, the gigantic building is always a simple, mostly angular tower, albeit of extraordinary height. It was not until the modern era, when the sciences were rapidly gaining in influence, that artists didn't merely continue in the tracks of their predecessors but took it upon themselves to seriously consider how such a colossal tower could actually have been constructed in the first place.

It was the Dutch painter Pieter Bruegel the Elder who produced epochal depictions of the scene with his two versions of the Tower of Babel from 1563. What makes these paintings so groundbreaking is the scientific thinking that informs his convincing mise en scène: his tower reveals itself as a massive, laborious construction site in the form of an enormous truncated cone, the top of which is already pushing up through the clouds yet obviously reaches much higher. A spiral ramp leads around the enormous body, on which we can see all sorts of tiny workers and cranes and construction materials being transported.

2 Gen. 11:1–9

Changing depictions of the Tower of Babel –
illustrations from the Old English Hexateuch (11th
c., above row, left to right), from the *Weltchronik
in Versen* (c.1370) and from the Bedford Hours
(1423). The painting by Pieter Bruegel the Elder
(1563) shook up representations of the tower
and its impact can still be felt today: versions by
Abel Grimmer (1595, above right), Marten van
Valckenborch (1595, centre right) and the 'New
Tower of Babel' in Fritz Lang's *Metropolis* (1927,
below left).

Bruegel travelled little and there is no indication that he was aware of the Samarra minaret. Yet there are astonishing similarities. In Bruegel's work, too, the ramp is both a means of transport and a processional route. The tower is shown – together with its laborious fabrication – in a way that has been generally accepted as realistic. This is perhaps not entirely due to the viability of its construction but may also have to do with the fact that the spiral is seen as the most dignified connection between God and humanity. Further, Bruegel's attention to detail effectively illustrates the megalomania involved and the impossibility of the undertaking. These paintings made it difficult to imagine any other way of depicting the tower: since 1563 there have been almost no angular versions, with the vast majority of illustrations up to the present day depicting helical forms. A chronological survey of all the subsequent variants of the tower reveals the overwhelming influence of these two works by Bruegel, and how their fame slowly spread across Europe: from Dutch and Flemish masters, such as Hendrick van Cleve and Hans Bol (c.1580), to Athanasius Kircher (1679), François de Nome (1620) and Gustave Doré (1865), before finally filtering through into modernity and the new medium of film, where we find the New Tower of Babel dominating the skyline of Fritz Lang's *Metropolis* (1927) or the royal city of Minas Tirith spiralling around a conical mountain in Peter Jackson's film adaptation of *The Lord of the Ring*s (2001–3).

As in the history of painting, the spiral's shift from being a utilitarian form – deployed in the routing of heavy loads – to an emblem of ascent can also be found in architecture, where it appeared even earlier than in the other arts. As Friedrich Mielke, founder of scalology, noted, 'The medieval stair construction [in Europe] was obviously so much determined by the art of the turn that one could only think of a staircase as a spiral staircase, especially when it had to serve higher purposes.'[3] This tendency established itself first of all in sacred architecture, the most famous staircases being those in Ravenna's San Vitale (525–547) and Charlemagne's Palatine Chapel in Karlsruhe (790–805) – that is, only slightly later than Trajan's Column in Rome, which may well have initiated the trend.

In the Middle Ages, anyone with any kind of self-regard built their stairs in helical form: soon 'spiral staircases alone were destined to serve the ascent to the heights of nobility'.[4] The effect of the spiral staircases in the great 12th- and 13th- century pilgrimage

3   Friedrich Mielke, *Geistige Treppen: Treppen des Geistes* (Stamsried: Vögel, 2001), 63.
4   Mielke, *Geistige Treppen*, 63.

Magnificent spiral staircases are placed in front
of the façades as 'spiral stones': at Albrechtsburg
Castle, Meissen (15th c., above left), Hartenfels
Castle, Torgau (16th c., above right) and the Maison
de l'Iran student residence in Paris designed by
Claude Parent and André Bloc (1967, below).

Corkscrewing towards the sky: the spiral spires of
Francesco Borromini's Sant'Ivo alla Sapienza,
Rome (1642–64, above left) and Laurids de Thurah's
Church of Our Saviour, Copenhagen (1689–1752,
above centre) and the spire of Strasbourg Cathedral
with 52 symbolic spiral staircases (above right)
with the modern interpretation by Philip Johnson
for the Chapel of Thanksgiving (1973–76) in Dallas,
Texas (below)

churches, such as those in Prague and Cologne, can hardly be over-estimated: both travellers and pilgrims spread enthusiastic tales of what they had seen. In the building of castles all over Europe, ambitious princes tried to outdo each other in their construction of ever more magnificent spiral staircases, one of the most elaborate examples being the double spiral staircase in the castle of Graz from 1499. The pair of particularly elaborate spiral staircases at the princely castles in Meissen (1471) and Bad Torgau (1535) were conspicuously placed in open stairwells in front of their respective courtyard façades, where they functioned as exhibits – tokens of the education and artistry of the princes and symbols of their power. They created an architectural motif that, like Bruegel's *Tower of Babel* in the discipline of painting, was to reverberate in architecture through the centuries. Even 500 years later in 1967, Claude Parent placed a radically modernised version of these helical stone staircases in front of his façade for the Maison de l'Iran in Paris – to serve as a fire escape. The spiral staircase that Francesco Borromini attached to his Church of San Ivo alla Sapienza in Rome prior to 1660 enjoyed a similarly potent impact. Here, the lantern atop the dome was transformed into a triple-spiralled walkable helix, an ornate structure that winds up into the infinity of the heavens. This motif found its continuation in 1752 in the Church of Our Saviour in Copenhagen and in the Chapel of Thanksgiving designed by the confirmed atheist Philip Johnson for Dallas, Texas, in 1976. Although Johnson's helix cannot be walked upon, the dynamic of its interior spiral and the symbolism of its colourful stained-glass ceiling effectively guide both eye and mind upwards to infinity, towards heaven, towards God.

Modern ascents: From temples and churches to museums and planetaria

The development of helical staircases in secular architectural history is hardly less spectacular, leading over the centuries from the spiral stairs of European princes' castles via the revolutionary architecture of Étienne-Louis Boullée more or less directly to Vladimir Tatlin's unbuilt Monument to the Third International from 1919. Tatlin described his design as an 'anti-monument', as revolutionary Russia's demonstrative counter-proposal to the monuments of the imperial era – such as the Eiffel Tower and the

American Statue of Liberty. His monument would indeed have outshone them all: a publicly accessible double spiral of steel that was to rise 400 meters above St Petersburg. Precisely because Tatlin's tower was never constructed, its historical impact had to depend entirely on its striking, and memorable, graphic representations. The prevalence of the tower's design announced the arrival of the helix as a fundamental architectural form in the modern era.

Meanwhile, in the early modernist period the spiral was an ideal response to the desire for a new, dynamic architecture that would reflect technological progress: the ramps that had been used in antiquity and the Middle Ages for horses and cannon were now redesigned for cars and lorries. However, like the stairways for bringing up heavy loads in Mesopotamian ziggurats, these typically remained concealed within their structures, the most impressive example being FIAT's revolutionary car factory in Lingotto, Turin, from 1916. Company president Giovanni Agnelli, who had visited the progressive Ford factories in the USA and wanted to bring them to Italy, appointed the local architect Giacomo Mattè-Trucco to design the factory. Mattè-Trucco organised the 500-metre-long building as a continuous production line, with all levels connected by smooth, curving ramps. The raw materials were delivered on the ground floor, and the cars were then sequentially completed floor by floor. From the fifth and final floor a freight lift delivered the finished cars to the roof, where they underwent their first test drive on a kilometre-long track that had a pair of banked curves at its gable ends. In Lingotto, it was no longer man ascending to God, but the car.

However, the exterior of the factory revealed nothing about the inner dynamics of production – from the outside, the factory is no more than a plain, rectangular box, albeit of inordinate length, with endless rows of windows. Nevertheless, Le Corbusier, one of the first visitors to the building, was thrilled by it, so much so that in 1923, the same year the factory went into operation, he used three photographs of it to cap his *Vers une architecture*.[5] Le Corbusier, too, had occasionally used ramps in his designs, but his interest in these architectural devices intensified dramatically following his visit to Turin. Ever more frequently, he added a second, alternative system for moving through the building located next to the 'normal' stairs, as was the case, for example, in the Villa Savoye, which he designed in 1929. In addition to this, he repeatedly made the ramp a component of his so-called 'promenades architecturales', in which the

5   See Wolfgang Pehnt, 'Automobilmachung: Zur Geschichte einer Fasczination', in *Die Erfindung der Geschichte: Aufsätze und Gespräche zur Architektur unseres Jahrhunderts* (Munich: Prestel, 1989), 87–104.

Vladimir Tatlin's 'Monument to the Third International' for St Petersburg (above right); Giacomo Matté-Trucco's 500-metre-long Fiat factory (1916–23) in Lingotto, whose spiral ramp is hidden inside (below); Le Corbusier in a Fiat 508 S Balilla on the test track on the roof of the factory, 1934 (above left)

ramps were no longer delivery or secondary routes but were instead conceived of as equal – if not more significant – elements of vertical circulation.[6] While straight staircases tend to create efficient, functional and therefore more mundane connections between two floors, Le Corbusier's ramps are a pleasure to walk along, offering engaging vistas and an overview of the building and its setting.

As in Turin, however, Le Corbusier's ramps usually have no effect on the exterior design of his buildings. They do not serve to determine the form of the structure, as they do in Samarra, nor are they spiral sculptures positioned in front of the building as in Meissen or Torgau. It was not until he was designing museums that Le Corbusier developed the spiral into a fundamental organisational figure: in 1929, at the invitation of Paul Otlet and Patrick Geddes, the architect designed the utopian Mundaneum in Geneva as a modernist temple precinct with an archaic flair, where the most important objects and documents drawn from the whole of human history and selected by an international organisation were to be preserved. The core building of the complex would have been the Musée mondial, a kind of meta-museum in which the chosen objects were to be presented in an exhibition that would be constantly updated. Le Corbusier designed the museum as a highly symbolic, angular stepped pyramid, which he termed a 'ziggurat' in one of his drawings.[7] The visitor would have first climbed the structure via the outer stairs – just as in the ancient models – with each plateau offering a new view of the world and an ever-increasing understanding, right up to the topmost level. Only here would the more comfortable descent have begun through the interior of the pyramid, where in chronological order the history of all human cultures would have been represented via objects and works of art.[8] Le Corbusier explained that the ever-greater length of the circuit as the path descended would allow more and more space for the exhibits inside, thus making it possible to present narratives with increasing scope and detail covering the period from prehistory to the present day. The gallery was intended as a continuous interior space that was constantly expanding downwards in a more or less smooth progression.

Le Corbusier never let go of this idea of a museum organised as a spiral that could be extended into infinity, as it were. He continued it in several idealised designs for a *Musée à croissance*

6   See Elisabeth Blum, *Le Corbusiers Wege: Wie das Zauberwerk in Gang gesetzt wird* (Braunschweig: Vieweg, 1988).
7   Paul Otlet and Le Corbusier, *Mundaneum: Exposé général et projet architectural* (Brussels: Union of International Associations, 1928).
8   Blum, *Le Corbusiers Wege*.

Competition for the first helical museum:
Le Corbusier's unrealised design for
the Mundaneum in Geneva (1929, above);
Frank Lloyd Wright's unrealised design
for the Gordon Strong Automobile Objective
on Sugarloaf Mountain (1924–29, below)

Frank Lloyd Wright's preliminary designs for
the Guggenheim Museum in New York (1943–44
above); Wright, Hilla Rebay and Solomon R.
Guggenheim next to the 1945 presentation model
(below)

illimitée – a Museum of Unlimited Growth – which he proposed for Paris in 1931. Here his idea is a one-storey, quadrangular or rectangular building with an angular spiral inside: 'The quadrangular spiral,' Le Corbusier wrote, 'which, starting in the central space, allows a break in the circuit (unlike the circular spiral), something that is desirable for visitors.' In total, more than ten such designs can be found in his complete works between 1930 and 1965 – during which period he even tried to patent the idea.[9] Le Corbusier was able to realise three of his designs based on spirals: the Sanskar Kendra Museum in Ahmedabad (1951–56), the Government Museum in Chandigarh (1952–68), and, lastly, the National Museum of Western Art in Tokyo (1957–59). In his Berlin lecture series of 1964, Oswald Mathias Ungers concluded that the Mundaneum plan was 'one of the most interesting designs not only within Le Corbusier's oeuvre but also within new architecture in general',[10] the spiral referring both to the infinity of human history and to the Tower of Babel.

What is surprisingly missing from Ungers's typological analysis is any reference to Frank Lloyd Wright, whose Guggenheim Museum in New York is probably the world's most famous monument to the spiral as a fundamental way of organising architecture. Like Le Corbusier, Wright had been involved with the spiral years earlier, and in fact there are several direct points of contact with Le Corbusier's work. In 1924, Wright had designed a curious lookout for American investor Gordon Strong in the shape of a giant snail shell to be positioned on top of Sugarloaf Mountain in Maryland. Having purchased the mountain and had a road laid out with a few parking bays, the enterprising businessman had given thought to ways of attracting more visitors: the mountain needed an attraction. Strong asked Wright, who suggested a large planetarium and went on to design a building which he developed directly from the road that snaked up the mountain by transforming it into a double spiral at the top. Cars would have driven up via the upper lane and down via the lower lane: a modern, drive-in, double spiral of a ziggurat that would have led guests in the greatest possible comfort to the entrance of the planetarium on the uppermost level. But Strong did not take kindly to Wright's idea, saying the structure was completely unspecific as it could be located on any hill. In his dismissive letter of 1925 he even enclosed an illustration of Pieter Bruegel's *Tower of Babel* just in case, Strong sneered, the painting was still missing from Wright's collection.[11]

9   Gregory Grämiger, 'Eckige Schnecke', in *trans 29: Ecke / Edge / Angle* (Zurich: gta Verlag, 2016), 51.
10 Oswald Matthias Ungers, 'Vorlesung 3, Wintersemester 1964/65', in 'Architekturlehre: Berliner Vorlesungen 1964–65', *Arch+* 179 (2006): 111.
11 For a more detailed account, see Mark Reinberger, 'Architecture in Motion: The Gordon Strong Automobile Objective', 4 Nov. 2019, https://franklloyd-wright.org/architecture-in-motion-the-gordon-strong-automobile-objective/.

Four years later Wright wrote to Strong with the intention of re-claiming his drawings: 'It appears that something similar is being considered over in France, only there it involves a museum. There has been some recent interest in this idea that I have worked out for you, and I have been asked several times to let the thing be seen.'[12] This museum 'over in France' was almost certainly Le Corbusier's Musée mondial. But there is nothing in Wright's estate about any further work on his designs for Sugarloaf Mountain. Perhaps Strong never did return the drawings.

Wright did not continue working intensively with the spiral again until 1943, when Hilla von Rebay asked him for a design for the Guggenheim Museum. Wright developed his basic spatial concept at lightning speed, summarising it in January 1944: 'The museum should be a single elongated floor space,... extending from top to (bottom), so that a wheelchair can, as it were, pass through it without interruptions all around.'[13] The idea of an uninterrupted ramp as a central internal figure, as in Le Corbusier's work, was fixed from the beginning and its development can be seen in a series of drawings that Wright made between 1943 and 1944: first he tested variants with square or octagonal ground plans that stacked up into ziggurat-like towers. This quickly developed into a circular, curved structure, which Wright – like Corbusier with the Mundaneum – marked, in his own hand, as a 'ziggurat' on the plans. In Wright's case, too, the intention was that visitors should first reach the top floor in comfort using a lift and then continue on down in a smooth progression, taking a leisurely route through the exhibition all the way to the ground floor.

More recent 'flights of knowledge'

However, the museum designs of Le Corbusier and Frank Lloyd Wright correspond in another, essential point: both are concerned with archaic typologies as important reference points for modern architecture. Ancient temples and places of worship as well as the highlights of royal castles and churches now become public muse-ums and planetaria – places dedicated to knowledge and research. As in William Blake's *Jacob's Dream*, we are no longer approaching the gods, but (self)knowledge. The destination may be different, but the journey's dramatic mise en scène remains. These two worlds collided with maximum force in the general remodelling of the Vatican Museums in 1932, where the architect Giuseppe Momo

---

12   Quoted in Reinberger, 'Architecture in Motion'.
13   Quoted in Bruce Brooks Pfeiffer, 'A Temple of Spirit', in *The Solomon R. Guggenheim Museum* (New York: Guggenheim Museum, 1994), 6.

introduced a central, double-intertwined spiral staircase as a spectacular, central element. On the very slow way either down or up, another motif was added in addition to the aspects of leisure and contemplation for the visitors: that of seeing and being seen. This too was to become a recurring topos: one of the world's best-known and most visited examples is I. M. Pei's 1989 remodelling of the Louvre and his generous, free-standing spiral staircase, which dominates the space beneath the glass pyramid.

Another mise en scène of a staged human ascent towards knowledge can be found in Paris, barely two kilometers from the Louvre. Back in 1977 the Centre Georges-Pompidou was opened, the pioneering temple of high-tech architecture par excellence, designed by Renzo Piano, Richard Rogers and Gianfranco Franchini. The building itself is a relatively restrained rectangular volume – albeit made of glass and steel – and this alone forms a strong contrast to its (historic) urban surroundings. Although this time not in helical from, the vertical access has been staged in a highly visible manner – as have all the technical installations. The main elevation facing onto the (newly formed) sloping public square is clearly accentuated by an impressive cascade of escalators encased in perspex. Their positioning and their particular design elevate these mundane means of transport from a simple technological tool to an architectural statement. Not only do the multiple bends of the cascade emphasise the presence of the six floors behind them, the transparency of the envelope allows the circulation of people through the entire structure to become the theme of the façade – and indeed of the building as a whole. This is symbolic in several ways: this piece of architecture – a public, educational institution – can be read as a simple tool designed to serve people, its interior space capable of being radically changed at any time in response to current needs. Moreover, its exterior displays human movement itself as the meaning, purpose and fuel of the 'machine'.

Such staging might be reminiscent of the ziggurats and stepped temples, but unlike their staircases, this contemporary version of ascent is no longer reserved for those who have been sanctified or ordained, but is freely accessible to everyone. The Centre Pompidou is a transparent building without hidden chambers, secrets or hierarchy: the modern path to knowledge is no longer dependent on the laborious ascent of one level after another. Visitors can decide for themselves how high they want to glide up the escalators.

The Centre Pompidou in Paris by Renzo Piano, Richard Rogers and Gianfranco Franchini (1972–77, above); the dome on the Reichstag in Berlin by Foster + Partners (1995–99, centre left) and the spiral staircase in the extension of the German Historical Museum in Berlin by I. M. Pei (1998–2003, centre right); the double spiral staircase (1932, below left) by Giuseppe Momo in the Vatican Museums; and the 500-metre-long helical staircase in London City Hall by Foster + Partners (1998–2002, below right)

The Centre Pompidou also established a distinctive architectural motif which would be carried forward. In his subsequent designs, Richard Rogers made the automated movements of lifts – and the staging of vertical human movement – a recurring theme in his architecture. His compatriot Norman Foster, who also likes to turn elements of building technology into expressive architectural elements, likewise developed a series of public buildings whose central motifs evolved from the staging of circulation. Unlike Rogers, Foster exploits the symbolism of the spiral – for example, in his design for the conversion of the German Reichstag in Berlin: here, on the roof of the massive, stone building designed in 1884 by Paul Wallot, he placed a publicly accessible glass dome containing an emphatically light spiral ramp. The transparency of democracy is quite literally translated into transparent architecture: as visitors descend the spiral route, their gaze reaches right down into the plenary chamber itself. The same motif is utilised in the architect's 1998–2002 design for London's City Hall, in which a formidable foyer is dominated by an equally formidable spiral ramp. At night, the transparency of the glass façades shows off the ramp's sculptural silhouette to the surrounding cityscape.

However, there is a particular overlap between the Centre Pompidou and the work of Foster, Rogers and I. M. Pei: none of their choreographed ascents has been designed as a structural element – that is, they have little effect on the forms of buildings they serve, their supporting structures or their internal spatial organisation. One could simply replace the ramps in Pei's extension to the Louvre and on the top of the Reichstag, or the escalators on the façade of the Centre Pompidou, with different means of vertical access – the essential, load-bearing structure of the respective buildings would remain unchanged.

The architectural promenades of OMA and their legacy

This issue is handled differently in the designs of the Office for Metropolitan Architecture, or OMA. Their architecture repeatedly works with ideas of circulation that draw heavily on those of Le Corbusier: architectural promenades are deployed through their buildings that function as spatial backbones. OMA's preoccupation with this theme can be seen over many years, as in the designs from 1989 for a ferry terminal in Zeebrugge and in 1989 and 1992 for a pair of libraries in Paris, as well as in the Public Library in Seattle,

The Dutch Embassy in Berlin by OMA (1997–2003, above left and right); OMA's design for the Jussieu Library in Paris (competition 1992, unrealised, centre left and right); Antwerp's Museum aan de Stroom (MAS) by Neutelings Riedijk (1999–2010, below)

which opened in 2004. In these projects, visitors are guided through the buildings along paths that become the defining, all-pervasive, spaces of movement, which are consistently made visible on the outside in a deliberate act of staging. In no realised design by OMA has this theme been more apparent than in the Dutch Embassy in Berlin, constructed at almost the same time as the Seattle Library. In Berlin, a 200-metre-long path leads from the entrance on the ground floor through all levels in a labyrinthine zigzag that unexpectedly changes direction again and again to end in the restaurant on the roof terrace. This route is sometimes a ramp, sometimes a staircase, sometimes flat, sometimes steep, and sometimes it even leads through the middle of the building to then emerge as a glass bridge in front of the façade. This is a completely different kind of visibility than, for example, at the Centre Pompidou. Instead of complete and sober transparency, in this case the views through are always only partial, presumably in order to leave room for the building's secrets.

The ideas that OMA put back on the contemporary architectural agenda were continued by a number of OMA employees when, in due course, they subsequently founded their own offices. These include Dutch architects Willem Jan Neutelings and Michiel Riedijk. One of their most spectacular buildings is the Museum aan de Strom, which opened in Antwerp in 2010. This new structure was a prestige project for the city, which wanted an iconic piece of architecture that would signal the transformation of a former industrial port area into a mixed residential and business district. Neutelings Riedijk's building is a 62-metre-high free-standing tower, whose façade comprises areas of reddish sandstone that alternate with those of floor-to-ceiling glazing. In section, the tower reveals itself as a relatively simple stack of two-storey enclosed exhibition spaces, each with a glazed foyer. This floor plan is rotated 90 degrees on each level, resulting in a promenade that constantly circles around the building's core. The angular spiral provides an ever-changing view of the city and turns the visitors' circulation into the most visible aspect of the building and thus its dominant architectural expression.

Like Jan Willem Neutelings, Matthias Sauerbruch also began his career at OMA. Sauerbruch Hutton's oeuvre includes a handful of designs for buildings whose helical routes form their basic architectural theme, long before Experimenta was conceived. In 1994, they proposed a design for the centre of Marzahn, a suburb of the former East Berlin, involving a structure, almost 3 kilometres in length, that would enable various traffic flows to converge in a new, centrally located department store. The structure itself comprised two intertwining spiral ramps, one of which was to have been reserved for vehicles and the other for the various retail areas of the large store. Convenient transitions from parking the car to shopping would have been possible at every level, the pair of spirals becoming a three-dimensional continuation and intensification of Marzahn's modernist urban landscape.

In a similar way, in 2001 Sauerbruch Hutton's competition design for BMW Welt (BMW World) in Munich adopted the flows of movement in the area surrounding the actual site and connected them into a centre comprising three arenas. In keeping with the project brief, the visitor (or employee) could have driven through the expansive project along a variety of routes. Sauerbruch Hutton have also developed spiral solutions for pedestrians, firstly for a market in Madrid (2007), where the helical path emerged from the topography of its site. And more recently, the theme was taken up again in 2008 in their design for the Munch Stenerson Museum in Oslo. Here a tower-like, sculptural building sits in an exposed position in the harbour basin. The museum tower was to comprise three stacked volumes in which the various departments of the collections would have been displayed. The visitor's path was to lead around the tower as an ascending spiral, opening up again and again to specific panoramas looking across the city and the sea. In retrospect, this unrealised design can perhaps be read as a preliminary study for Experimenta. However, Heilbronn's spiral route, which offers views over both the landscape and the city, is also employed as a deliberate device to define an extremely clear arrangement of spaces and thus – together with its specifically developed experimental structure – is instrumental in tying the various parts into an organic whole.

While the new Experimenta building is an original structure that was entirely developed from its site and its brief, it can also be linked to a long genealogy that leads via OMA to the Centre Pompidou, to Le Corbusier's Mundaneum and Frank Lloyd Wright's Sugarloaf Mountain, to Jacob's Ladder, the Tower of Babel and the minaret in Samarra, Trajan's Column and even the ziggurats of Mesopotamia. The ancient, traditional themes of mankind's architectural and cultural history embedded in these structures are vividly continued in the new building. As a result, Experimenta itself has now become a small part of this age-old narrative of man's longing to ascend to knowledge, to light.

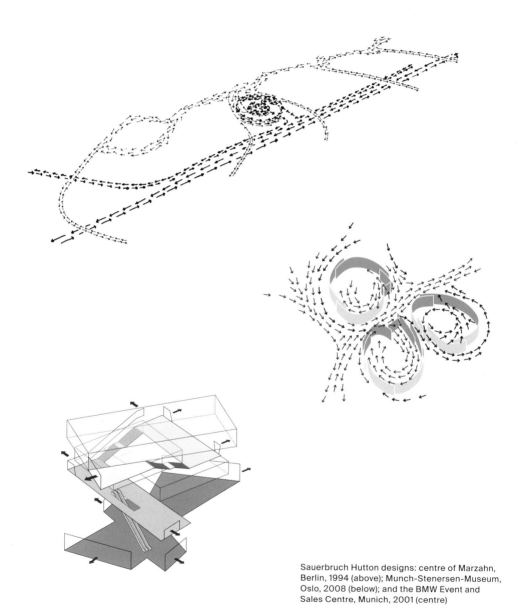

Sauerbruch Hutton designs: centre of Marzahn, Berlin, 1994 (above); Munch-Stenersen-Museum, Oslo, 2008 (below); and the BMW Event and Sales Centre, Munich, 2001 (centre)